Official Annual 2013
CONTENTS

A Year of Excitement

Everything you're about to read is highly confidential. A group of penguins worked in secret in 2012 to make sure Club Penguin and its citizens were safe. These secret agents faced huge danger in doing so. You may have been one of these agents!

Welcome to the classified world of the Elite Penguin Force, a Secret Agency that protects Club Penguin. Do you have what it takes to be an EPF agent?

TOP SECRET

Becoming an EPF Agent

If you're not already an Elite Penguin Force agent, you'll need a top secret invitation from another agent. This message will take you to the Everyday Phoning Facility, located in the Ski Village. When the phone rings, answer it. You'll be tested on your aim, speed, stealth and problem-solving skills. Don't worry if you don't pass the test the first time. You can take it as many times as you need.

You'll be made an Elite Penguin Force agent when you pass the test. Then you'll be given a Spy Phone and allowed access to the EPF Command Room.

The Director: Always in the shadows, no one knows for sure the real identity of the Director of the EPF.

G: Otherwise known as Gary the Gadget Guy, Club Penguin's inventor creates gadgets for the EPF too.

TOP SECRET

The EPF Team
They've got your back! The EPF protects Club Penguin from all threats, the biggest of which is Herbert P. Bear (along with his sidekick, Klutzy the Crab). As an agent, you'll work with G, the Director, Dot, Rookie, Jet Pack Guy and PH to put a stop to Herbert's latest plans.

The History of the EPF
Secret agents used to work out of the Penguin Secret Agency Headquarters until Herbert, a polar bear determined to destroy Club Penguin, trashed the HQ with a giant popcorn machine. The EPF had to step in and take over secret agent operations. Now, all agents work for the EPF.

An Agent's Duty
All agents work undercover and never reveal their identity. Agents are always on the lookout for signs of trouble and are encouraged to help other penguins around the island.

If the EPF has a mission for you, they will contact you through your Spy Phone. Report for duty in the Command Room, where you'll get your orders for Field-Ops. It's also where you can take on System Defender to protect Club Penguin.

PH: The elite puffle trainer. If you're working on a case that involves puffles, PH can help!

Jet Pack Guy: You'll recognize him from his sunglasses and the jet pack strapped to his back.

Dot: A master of disguise, she could be standing right in front of you and you might not even know it!

Rookie: He's always eager to protect the island, even if he does make a few mistakes.

Elite Gear

You're an agent. Now you have to look the part! When you complete an EPF Field-Op, or stop a threat in System Defender, you'll receive a medal. Use these medals to buy outfits and accessories only available to agents. Click on the Elite Gear icon on your Spy Phone to get started on your super-secret shopping spree!
Be a specialist! Agents can develop their strength and skills, as well as buy and wear outfits for the different agent classes: Comm, Tactical, Tech and Stealth.

Starter Gear:
Delta and Alpha

Pick up the Delta fedora, shades, suit and sneaks to look your agent best. Or choose the Alpha wig, shades, suit and pumps.

Don't forget an earpiece! EPF, Delta and Alpha styles are available.

6

Tech

Tech agents are the brains of the EPF. They use their technological know-how to shut down enemy defences, computers and security systems. Look like the smartest agent in the room with your Optic Headset, Tech Coat, Tech Satchel and Tech-Book 3000.

Comm

Comm agents are communication experts. They intercept enemy intelligence, jam signals and maintain communication with Command. Help find the enemy and bring them down with the Comm Helmet, Sat-Pack, Comm Gear and Comm Boots.

Stealth

Stealth agents go behind enemy lines to win battles. You'll be able to infiltrate the enemy and sharpen your spy skills with the Dark Vision Goggles, Blue Power Cell, Canister Camouflage and Sneak-ers.

Tactical

Tactical agents are known as the swords and shields of the EPF. Their advanced high-impact armour can shrug off damage. Protect yourself with the H20 Pack, Range Finder, Tactical Gear and Tactical Boots.

Spy Skills

To keep Club Penguin safe, agents need tip-top memories, keen powers of observation and problem-solving skills. They've also got to be able to think fast on their feet. To keep these talents sharp, agents need to practise. You'll find activities throughout this book that will help improve your EPF agent skills. Whenever you visit Club Penguin, be sure to visit the Command Room regularly to keep your agent abilities at their best.

Field-Ops

Each week, a new Field-Op is released. You'll get a message on your phone letting you know when there is a new one. Report to the Command Room and waddle over to the big screen on the right side of the room. G will let you know what your assignment is. Past Field-Ops have included searching for and destroying enemy machinery, finding and fixing EPF gadgets, and looking for enemy signals. Be sure to do each new Field-Op to keep your spy skills sharp.

System Defender

Defend the EPF mainframe computer in System Defender. Once you've mastered the training program, you can move on to the advanced Elite Training Program. You'll learn how to build defensive cannons to protect the computer in case of an attack. It will put your problem-solving skills to the test!

SYSTEM DEFENDER

NO THREATS DETECTED

TUTORIAL

ADVANCED

FIELD-OPS

STATUS
[STANDING BY]

YOUR ORDERS:

Assigned by:

G
TECHNOLOGY SPECIALIST

The Herbert investigation has hit a dead end. We have no idea where Herbert is. So we're going to try something different. Go to the EPF antenna on top of the Ski Hill, and broadcast a message. Lock onto Herbert's phone, and ask if he is all right.

ACCEPT FIELD-OP

TUBE TRANSPORT

VIRUS SCANNER

FIELD-OPS

ELITE PENGUIN FORCE

Teamwork Counts!
Always remember, the best way for penguins to complete their assignments is to work together. You'll need all of your agent skills to succeed in the EPF - but you'll also need your friends!

Spot the Differences

Put your powers of observation to the test. Look at these two pictures of EPF agents and villains. Fifteen things have been changed in the picture on the right. See if you can spot and circle all the differences.

Mystery Maze

Herbert has captured you! The only way to escape - and put a stop to Herbert's plans - is to find the key and free yourself. Watch out for Herbert, Klutzy and traps along the way!

Put Your Memory to the Test

Agents need to have a good memory. Study this picture carefully for twenty seconds. Then turn the page and see how many questions you can answer correctly without peeking!

Put Your Memory to the Test

1 How many penguins are pictured?

Three

2 What game are the penguins playing?

Mancala

3 What colour is the penguin who is sitting on the floor?

orangE

4 Which penguin is wearing sandals?

The Blue one

5 What colour is the sofa?

Red

6 How many legs does the stool have?

four

7 Does the orange penguin look happy or grumpy?

happy

8 How many penguins are wearing glasses?

Two

9 Are there any puffles in the picture?

No

BONUS QUESTION:
What colour is the rug underneath the sofa?

Red

Puffle Puzzle

Test your deduction skills with this puffle puzzle. Colour in the puffles so that yellow, red, purple, green, blue and pink puffles appear once in each row, column and 3x2 box. Use logic and elimination to succeed.

A Mix-Up in the Mine

"It's pretty cool that the Director sent us on this case together, right?" Rookie asked. "I mean, it's like we're a team. Partners, almost."

Elite Penguin Force agents Rookie and Jet Pack Guy were waddling across the snow-covered ground to their next assignment. Both penguins were secret agents, but they couldn't have looked more different. Rookie was a green penguin with a red-and-white propeller cap on his head and red sunglasses. Jet Pack Guy, a red penguin, looked more professional in his dark suit, crisp white shirt and grey tie. His eyes couldn't be seen behind his black wrap-around sunglasses, and he wore a jet pack on his back, ready to spring into action at a moment's notice.

Jet Pack Guy stopped in his tracks. "Let's get one thing straight, Rookie," he said in his gruff voice. "We are not partners. Get it?"

"Oh yeah, of course," Rookie said quickly as Jet Pack Guy started to move again. "I just mean it's cool that we're working together. You and me. Rookie and Jet Pack Guy.

The R to the J-P-G. Me and you —"

"Don't get too excited, kid," Jet Pack Guy warned. "This seems like a pretty simple case. We should be out of here in a few minutes."

The two agents stopped in front of the entrance to the Mine, a craggy cave that descended into Club Penguin's underground.

Inside, a small group of concerned penguins had gathered at the start of the mine cart tracks that led deep into the shaft. Jet Pack Guy made his way into the middle of the crowd.

"Step aside, step aside!" he said in a commanding voice, and the chatting penguins quietened down as he passed. Behind him, Rookie was doing his best to sound as professional as his fellow agent.

"That's right, clear a path, please!" he said. "We're on official EPF business here!"

Jet Pack Guy nodded to a yellow penguin with curly brown hair.

"Ma'am, can you please tell me what seems to be the problem?" he asked.

"Well, one of the mine carts broke down inside the shaft," she replied. "And now no one can play Cart Surfer."

"Did you notice any unusual activity in the mine before the cart broke down?" Jet Pack Guy asked the crowd.

The penguins spoke to each other in low tones, trying to remember. A brown penguin spoke up first.

"No," he said. "Why? Should we have?"

"Just asking," Jet Pack Guy replied.

A purple penguin narrowed his eyes suspiciously. "Hey, why did the EPF send two agents to investigate a broken mine cart? Isn't that a job for Gary the Gadget Guy?"

"Normally it would be," Rookie told him. "But Agent G has uncovered some evidence that Herbert the evil Polar Bear is plotting something, and he wanted us to make sure that this isn't a – hmph!"

Jet Pack Guy clamped his flipper around Rookie's beak. "What Agent Rookie meant to say is that this is standard procedure. Nothing to worry about here. Right, Rookie?"

Rookie slowly nodded, and Jet Pack Guy removed his flipper. "Right!" Rookie said. "Standard procedure in case of suspicious activi – hmph!"

Jet Pack Guy shut Rookie's beak once again. "There's nothing more to see here, folks."

The penguins looked disappointed, but they slowly began to waddle away.

Rookie wriggled out of Jet Pack Guy's grip. "Hey, what was that all about? I was just telling them what G said about Herbert."

Ever since he had washed up on the island, the villainous polar bear had made it his mission to warm up Club Penguin and get rid of those pesky agents.

MINE

With the help of allies like Klutzy the Crab and the Protobot, he had caused all kinds of trouble on Club Penguin – including earthquakes and avalanches!

"That's top secret," the other agent reminded him. "G doesn't want to alarm anyone on the island. We don't want anyone to panic. Got it?"

Rookie gave a smart salute. "Got it, JPG! Now let's do some investigating."

Jet Pack Guy sighed. "Please don't call me JPG."

He took a flashlight off his tool belt and shone it into the dark Mine. The beam of light glinted off a metal cart in the distance.

"That must be the broken cart," Jet Pack Guy said. "Let's check it out."

"Roger that!" Rookie said enthusiastically. He took a magnifying glass from his tool belt. "How about I comb the tunnel for clues?"

"Fine," Jet Pack Guy said as he waddled toward the cart. He bent down and started examining the axles and wheels. The front left wheel had tilted, and wasn't firmly on the track like the other three. On closer inspection he saw the problem: a loose bolt.

A few metres down the tunnel, Rookie was busy examining a stalactite with his magnifying glass. "There could be clues anywhere," he muttered.

"I think I know why the cart isn't working!" Jet Pack Guy called down to him.

In the echoing tunnel, Rookie didn't hear him correctly. "The cart is working? Super!" he cried, and then raced back to the Mine Cave.

"No, I said I think I know why it isn't working!" Jet Pack Guy repeated, but Rookie was too far away to hear him. The agent shook his head.

"Well, he gets an A+ for enthusiasm," Jet Pack Guy muttered to himself. "Although I wonder why he ran out like that?"

Then a rumbling sound began to echo through the tunnel. The sound grew louder and louder. Something was coming toward him!

Jet Pack Guy shone his flashlight down the shaft to see Rookie barrelling toward him in a mine cart at top speed.

"Woo hoo!" Rookie cried, balancing on the cart with just one flipper. "You're right, JPG! It's working great!"

"I said it's not working!" Jet Pack Guy yelled. "Rookie, stop!"

But Rookie couldn't hear him over the roar of the cart. Jet Pack Guy raced to meet the cart before it collided with the broken mine cart. With a flying leap he reached out and pulled the brakes on Rookie's speeding cart.

Creeeeeeeeeeeak! The cart's brakes squealed as they came to an abrupt stop. The force sent Rookie flying. He landed with a thud inside the broken cart.

Dazed, Rookie looked around. "Hey, I thought you said this was working."

Jet Pack Guy's face turned even more red than usual. "I said – never mind." He took a deep breath to calm himself. "The cart's still broken. But it doesn't look like foul play. A nut must have fallen off during a sharp turn. Now we've got a loose bolt on the front left wheel."

"Don't worry, I'll find it!" Rookie said. He pulled out his torch and headed back down the track. "I think I saw some stuff in this little cave over here!"

Jet Pack Guy sighed and began to scan the ground around the mine cart. He was sure the missing nut had to be nearby. But if Rookie wanted to go running off again, he knew nothing he could say would stop him.

The agent carefully moved his torch along the rocky floor of the cave, hoping to find the missing piece. He had circled the cart once when Rookie came running up, breathless.

"I found it!" he cried. "The missing nut!"

He placed a small, round piece of metal in Jet Pack Guy's flipper. The agent held it up to examine it and frowned.

"This isn't a nut," he said. "It's a cap. And there's something written on it. Let's see."

Jet Pack Guy aimed his flashlight at the cap: DANGER. REMOVING THIS SAFETY CAP MAY CAUSE EXPLOSION.

"Rookie, where did you get this?" Jet Pack Guy asked.

Rookie pointed down the track. "There's a little cave not far from here. There's a big metal can, and I saw this round piece of metal on top of it, so I grabbed it and brought it to you."

Jet Pack Guy looked worried. "Rookie, duck!"

Rookie looked around. "A duck? Where?"

Jet Pack Guy pushed Rookie down to the ground and fell beside him – just in time.

BOOM! An explosion rocked the Mine shaft. Tiny pieces of rock shot through the tunnel and a cloud of dust made it impossible to see for several minutes. When the dust cleared, Jet Pack Guy stood up and brushed off his suit.

"Rookie, are you okay?" he asked.

Rookie jumped up. "You bet!" he said. "Wow! That was a pretty cool explosion, wasn't it?"

Normally, Jet Pack Guy could remain calm in any situation. But all of his patience had vanished.

"No, Rookie!" he fumed. "Blowing up the Mine is not acceptable!"

Rookie looked deflated. "Sorry. I guess I get carried away sometimes."

"Come on," Jet Pack Guy said gruffly. "Let's go see what damage you've caused."

"Okay, JP–" Rookie stopped when Jet Pack Guy glared at him. "I mean, Jet Pack Guy."

They waddled to the site of the explosion, ducking into the small cave Rookie had found. A big hole had been blasted into the cave's back wall.

"We'll have to close the Mine until we can shore this up," Jet Pack Guy said with a frown. "We need to make sure everything's safe."

Rookie waddled to the hole and peered through it.

"Um, first you might want to call G," Rookie said.

"Why?" Jet Pack Guy asked.

Rookie motioned to him. "Check this out."

The hole opened up into another small cave – a secret one. This cave held all kinds of technical-looking equipment.

"Hey, isn't that a piece of the conveyor belt from Pizzatron 3000?" Rookie asked, pointing.

Jet Pack Guy nodded. "Sure looks like it. And that's the claw from the Aqua Grabber."

"And there's one of the cannons from Puffle Launch," Rookie said. "What's it all doing here?"

Jet Pack Guy looked thoughtful. "You're right, Rookie. We need to call G."

Rookie beamed and started to do a little dance. "He says I'm right! He says I'm right!"

Jet Pack Guy shook his head and pressed some buttons on his spy phone. "G, you'd better get to the Mine shaft right away."

Seconds later a blue penguin teleported into the tunnel. He wore round glasses, and a blue shirt and tie peeked out from beneath his white lab coat. Most penguins on the island knew him as Gary the Gadget Guy, the genius inventor who created games and devices such as the Clock Tower and Pizzatron 3000. But secret agents called him G, the Tech Lead for the EPF.

"Is everything all right, Jet Pack Guy?" Agent G asked. Then he noticed the hole in the cave and raised an eyebrow. "Oh, I see. There's been an explosion."

"That was, um, my fault, kind of, " Rookie admitted.

"That's not why we called you down here," Jet Pack Guy said. "Check out what's in there."

Gary approached the hole and looked inside. "Aha! Just as I suspected!"

"What do you mean, G?" Rookie asked.

The blue penguin turned to face the agents. "Over the last few weeks, pieces from my inventions have gone missing from all over the island. I didn't think anything of it at first, but when it kept happening I thought that Herbert must be behind it. I suspect he is gathering this technology to construct some new kind of dastardly device."

"Whoa," Rookie said. "That could have been bad!"

G smiled. "His stash of stolen goods has been discovered, thanks to you two agents! Good work!"

Rookie grinned and looked up at Jet Pack Guy. "Did you hear that? Gary said we did good work! I've got to remember to write that in my diary tonight."

"In fact," G went on, "you two make such a good team that I am going to recommend that the Director make you permanent partners. What do you think of that?"

Jet Pack Guy looked stunned for a second. Then he softened.

"I hate to admit it, but Rookie, I couldn't have done it without you," he said. He held up his flipper for a high-five.

Rookie jumped up and slapped his flipper. When he landed, he spun around and started his happy dance again. "Did you see that? Jet Pack Guy high-fived me. Me! This guy!" He stopped. "You're the best, JPG."

"Rookie, if we're going to be partners you've got to remember one thing," Jet Pack Guy said.

"What's that?" Rookie asked. "Never let the bad guy see you first? Always carry your Spy Phone? Eat a good breakfast every day?"

Jet Pack Guy shook his head. "No," he said. "The one thing you need to remember is to never, ever, call me JPG!"

23

Field-Ops

Your mission: gather up some friends and put your secret agent skills to the test! Make sure you ask a parent's permission before playing.

You Will Need:
- Four or more friends
- Paper and a pen to write down your plans
- Resourcefulness
- Flashlights, stopwatches and other spy gear are optional for this game

Your Orders:
- Create a list of secret agent Field-Ops to do with your friends (see examples opposite).
- Split your agents into teams and give each team the list of tasks.
- Set a time limit.
- Move out!
- The team that completes all Field-Ops first is victorious.

Operation Seek & Recover

Tools: A small bag for each team.

Objective: Team members will need to bring back a total of four objects from the field in the following shapes: one circle, one square, one triangle, and one rectangle.

Operation 'Touch' Down

Tools: A small bag for each team.

Objective: Team members need to find something fuzzy, something smooth, something bumpy and something scratchy.

Operation 'S' Marks the Spot

Tools: Paper and a pen for each team.

Objective: Bring back a list of fifteen things in the field that start with the letter "s".

There are no limitations to devising your own Field-Ops. Use your imagination to come up with more missions. And be sure to have an adult check your orders before your teams head out!

EPF Crossword

Use your puzzle-solving skills and everything you know about the EPF to crack this crossword!

Across:

5. Outfits and accessories only available to agents are found here. (5, 4)
6. No one knows this penguin's true identity. (8)
7. This polar bear is always causing trouble for agents. (7)
9. Every agent is issued this piece of equipment. (3, 5)
10. Build cannons as fast as you can to protect the EPF mainframe in this game. (6, 8)

Down:

1. The agency that protects Club Penguin and keeps it safe. (5, 7, 5)
2. Agents are sent out on this kind of mission every week. (5, 3)
3. Agents receive their orders from this inventor, also known as G. (4)
4. The headquarters where agents meet and get their assignments. (7, 4)
8. He's always eager to protect the island, even if he makes some mistakes along the way! (6)

Word Search

Use your detecting skills to find the answers from the EPF Crossword Puzzle in this word search.

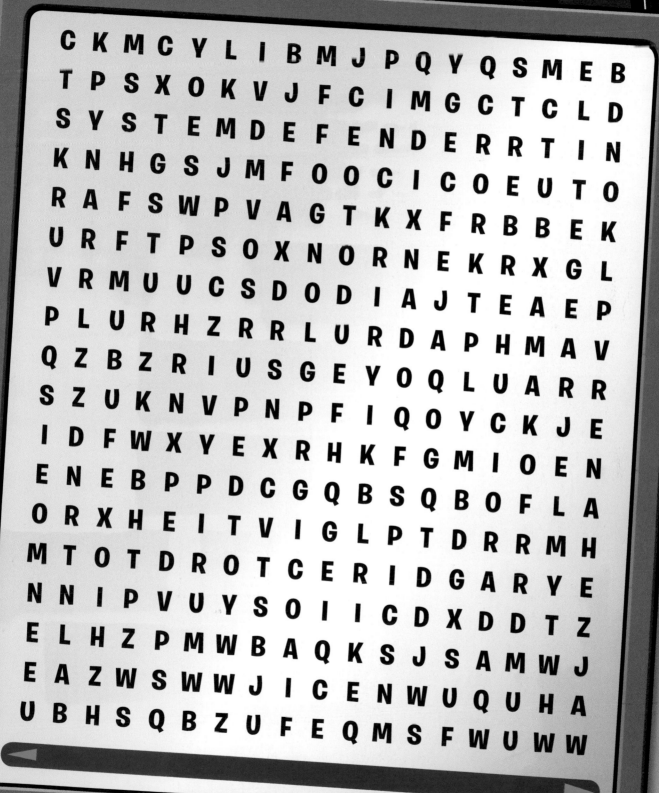

```
C K M C Y L I B M J P Q Y Q S M E B
T P S X O K V J F C I M G C T C L D
S Y S T E M D E F E N D E R R T I N
K N H G S J M F O O C I C O E U T O
R A F S W P V A G T K X F R B B E K
U R F T P S O X N O R N E K R X G L
V R M U U C S D O D I A J T E A E P
P L U R H Z R R L U R D A P H M A V
Q Z B Z R I U S G E Y O Q L U A R R
S Z U K N V P N P F I Q O V C K J E
I D F W X Y E X R H K F G M I O E N
E N E B P P D C G Q B S Q B O F L A
O R X H E I T V I G L P T D R R M H
M T O T D R O T C E R I D G A R Y E
N N I P V U Y S O I I C D X D D T Z
E L H Z P M W B A Q K S J S A M W J
E A Z W S W W J I C E N W U Q U H A
U B H S Q B Z U F E Q M S F W U W W
```

27

Agent Anagrams

Can you solve these tricky anagrams? An anagram is what you get when you take one word and rearrange the letters to make one or more new words from it. So, for example, if you take the letters in 'snow', you can make 'owns' or 'sown'.

Here are ten anagrams made from the names of penguins, places and things on Club Penguin. Rearrange the letters in the words to spell out one of the words in the word bank. Write the answers in the spaces below. Then write the letters in the blue shaded boxes in order on the spaces opposite to find out a secret message from The Director of the EPF.

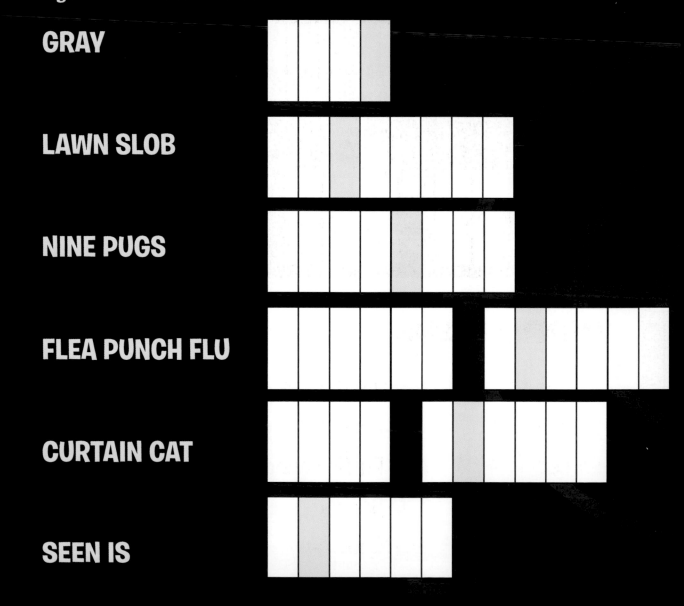

GRAY

LAWN SLOB

NINE PUGS

FLEA PUNCH FLU

CURTAIN CAT

SEEN IS

CHOICE KEY

SOFTER

FROST

EAGER TILE

The message from the Director of the EPF is:

        !

WORD BANK

Aunt Arctic   Ice Hockey

Elite Gear   Penguins

Forest   Puffle Launch

Forts   Sensei

Gary   Snowball

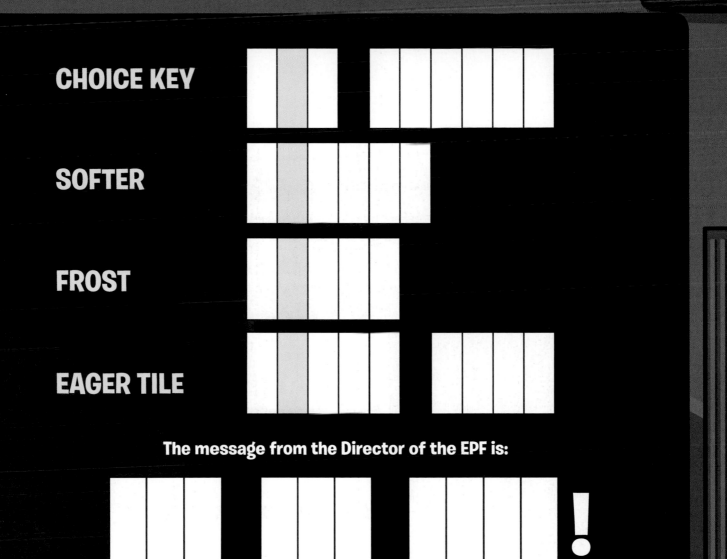

Pass Code Puzzle

A hidden computer signal has been detected on the island. To read it, you must decrypt the pass code. Can you work out the message and write it in the space below?

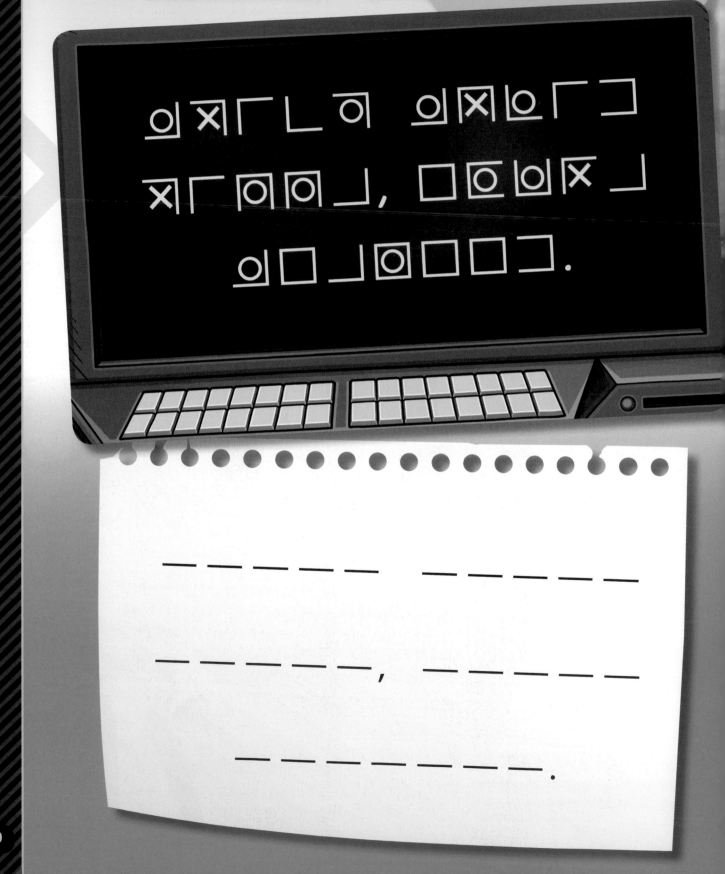

Secret Code

A =
B =
C =
D =
E =
F =
G =
H =
I =
J =
K =
L =
M =

N =
O =
P =
Q =
R =
S =
T =
U =
V =
W =
X =
Y =
Z =

Great job, agent! You managed to crack the code . . . although the message is highly unusual.

Oops! I was trying to order a snack and used the Comm Helmet instead of my phone. Sorry, G!

31

Masters of Disguise

Agents are great at disguising themselves. They also have to be good at seeing through the disguises of others! Do these famous penguins in costume fool you? Take a close look at the penguins below. Write down who you think each one really is in the space next to each picture. Good luck!

1

2

NAME BANK

Cadence   **Rockhopper**   **Aunt Arctic**

3

4

5

Gary the Gadget Guy   Sensei

Rookie and the Ruby

"Thanks for letting me help you, Gary!" Rookie said happily. "Your lab is really cool!"

Gary the Gadget Guy pushed his round glasses up on his beak. "I appreciate your help, Rookie. I am hoping to get this new popcorn machine ready for the next Fair. It pops popcorn twice as fast, you see, so that penguins won't have to wait in long queues."

Gary opened a drawer in the machine's metal base. "The popcorn goes in here, and then all you need to do is simply flick the switch to turn it on."

"I'll get the popcorn!" Rookie offered eagerly. He raced across the lab and came back with a huge, heavy sack.

"Be careful, Rookie," Gary warned. "That bag is heavy."

"I'll be – whoa!" Rookie cried, as he accidentally tripped over his own feet. The entire sack of popcorn kernels spilled into the machine as Rookie fell. He tried to steady himself by grabbing onto the nearest thing – the lever that turned on the machine.

"Oh dear," Gary said.

Pop! Pop! Pop! Pop! Pop! Pop! Pop! The machine started shooting out puffy white popcorn at an amazing speed. Gary tried to reach the lever, but a spray of popcorn smacked into him, knocking him back.

"I've got this!" Rookie yelled. He opened his beak and began to gobble up the popcorn as it shot out of the machine. Gary had just enough time to run to the lever and shut down everything.

"Well, that was interesting," Gary said, brushing popcorn kernels from his lab coat.

"I'm really sorry!" Rookie said. "I tripped."

"It's not a problem," Gary said kindly. "It's important to test the machine under all kinds of conditions. But I think I need to study this new data by myself, if you don't mind."

Rookie looked deflated. "Okay, Gary. Let me know if you need me, okay?"

The young agent left Gary's lab and headed to the Coffee Shop. He found a table by himself and began to write in his diary.

> Dear Diary,
> It looks like I've done it again! I really messed up when I was helping Gary with his popcorn machine. Gary said not to worry about it, but I felt bad. Why do I have to be so clumsy? I need to show the other agents and the Director that I can handle myself in the field. The next time G sends me out on a case, I'm going to impress everyone!
> Your friend,
> Rookie

Rookie put down his pen and took a sip of cocoa. Because he was an elite agent, Rookie always kept his eyes and ears open when he was in a public place. He listened to the scattered conversations going on around him.

"I'm telling you, it's possible to tip the Iceberg!"

"My new puffle did the cutest thing today . . ."

" . . . and then Miss Ruby said someone stole her ruby!"

Rookie snapped to attention. A stolen ruby? He waddled over to a table occupied by one red penguin and one orange penguin.

"Excuse me, but I overheard you talking about a stolen ruby," Rookie said. "Where did this happen?"

The two penguins looked confused.

"At The Stage, of course," replied the orange penguin.

"Stage. Got it! I'm on the case!" Rookie said, before rushing out onto the street.

He quickly waddled from the Town Center to the Plaza, where The Stage was nestled between the Pet Shop and the Pizza Parlor.

"This is my big chance!" he said as he made his way there. "I'll solve this missing ruby mystery by myself and impress everyone at the EPF!"

Rookie imagined standing in the EPF room, surrounded by agents as G gave him a medal.

"It was nothing," he would say modestly. "I got a lead and followed it, just like any good EPF agent should."

Rookie was so lost in his daydream that he didn't notice the sign above the door of the Stage. It read: 'Now Showing: Ruby and the Ruby'. Had he seen it, he might have figured out that the penguins in the Coffee Shop were talking about the plot of a play, and not a real stolen ruby. In the play, a penguin named Miss Ruby asks a detective named Jacques Hammer to help her find her missing gem.

Eager to solve the case, Rookie ran inside. The stage inside was set with scenery painted black-and-white.

"I wonder what play they're putting on here?" Rookie wondered as he walked up the aisle. "Well, that's not important. I've got to find this Miss Ruby so I can help her find her missing ruby."

Rookie approached a pink penguin who was pulling costumes out of a big, brown trunk.

"Excuse me," he said. "Can you please tell me where I can find Miss Ruby?"

"I think she's over there," the penguin said, pointing to a red penguin with blonde hair, wearing a sparkly red dress.

"Thanks!" Rookie said.

Miss Ruby was pacing back and forth on the stage, reading some script pages.

I guess she must be acting in this play, whatever it is, Rookie thought. I hope I find her ruby before opening night!

"Excuse me, Miss Ruby?" Rookie asked, tapping her on the shoulder.

Miss Ruby turned around. "Yes?" she asked, her blonde hair bouncing on her shoulders.

"I heard that you lost your ruby, and I'd like to help you find it," he said. "Mind if I ask you a few questions?"

Miss Ruby looked from side to side, puzzled. "Um, are you Jacques Hammer?" She nodded to Rookie's red-and-white propeller cap. "I thought you'd be dressed differently."

"I always wear this," said Rookie, tapping his cap. "And anyway, I'm Rookie. Who is this Hammer guy? Is he a suspect?"

Miss Ruby pointed across the stage, where a green penguin in a blue suit was leaning against the wall. "No, he's the suspect. That's Tenor."

Tenor was another character in the play, but Rookie didn't know that. He eyed the penguin suspiciously. In his shiny suit, Tenor looked like an old-fashioned gangster. Just the type to steal a valuable jewel.

"And when was the ruby stolen?" Rookie asked her.

"Last night," Miss Ruby replied.

"Gotcha!" Rookie said. "I won't let you down, Miss Ruby!"

Miss Ruby shook her head as Rookie raced across the stage to talk to Tenor.

"Excuse me, Mr. Tenor," he said. "I need to ask you some questions about Miss Ruby's missing ruby."

Tenor looked confused. "Um, are you Jacques Hammer? What's with the hat?"

"No, I'm Rookie," he replied. "Why does everyone keep asking me if I'm this Hammer guy? And what's wrong with my hat?"

"Nothing," Tenor said. He started flipping through the pages of his script. "Did things change or something? I don't see anything about a Rookie in here."

"That's because I just took the case," Rookie said. "And I'd like to ask you a few questions. Miss Ruby says you're a suspect. Come clean. Did you take her ruby?"

Tenor looked down at his script. "Um, I was right here with my Hopscotch Gang."

Tenor pointed to the floor, where a hopscotch board had been drawn with chalk.

"So you like to play hopscotch, huh?" Rookie asked. "Tell you what. I'll play you at hopscotch. If I win, you answer my questions. Okay?"

Tenor frowned. "I don't think it's supposed to go like this."

"Nervous, huh?" Rookie asked. "Tell you what. I'll do it blindfolded."

Tenor shrugged. "Whatever you say!"

Rookie pulled a scarf from a nearby costume trunk and walked up to the hopscotch board. Then he blindfolded himself, wrapping the scarf across his red sunglasses.

"Watch this!" Rookie called out.

He began to hop down the board, planting his feet in the numbered boxes. Even though he couldn't see, he completed the board expertly.

"How was that?" Rookie asked, pulling off his blindfold.

"Not bad," Tenor said, sounding impressed. "You didn't even step on any of the lines."

"So you'll answer my questions?" Rookie asked.

"Why not?" Tenor replied.

"Then tell me," Rookie said. "Did you steal Miss Ruby's ruby?"

"I didn't," Tenor said. "I told you, I was hanging with my Hopscotch Gang all night."

Rookie frowned. "You're sticking to your story, huh? I've got to think about this."

Rookie stepped to the side and tapped his foot anxiously, thinking.

"I've got no other leads," he said. "Maybe it's time I talked to this Jacques Hammer."

He looked around the stage and saw a door to an office marked "Jacques Hammer, Detective." Rookie walked to the door and stepped inside.

Hammer's office was black and white, just like the rest of the set. A green penguin wearing a trench coat and fedora hat sat behind a desk.

"I was working late. A terrible storm was raging," Jacques Hammer was saying. Then he looked up at Rookie in surprise. "Hey! You're not Miss Ruby."

"No, I'm Rookie," Rookie said. "Do you always talk to yourself like that?"

The actor playing Jacques Hammer looked at his script, confused. "Is there some kind of change or something?"

"Nothing's changed," Rookie replied. "Miss Ruby's ruby is still missing."

Hammer suddenly looked like he understood. "Oh, I get it! You're with the props department. You see, the ruby has been planted on the set, over by–"

"Planted? Got it!" Rookie said. "And you can give me my props later, after I find the ruby."

Rookie ran out of the office, and the first thing he spotted was a potted plant on a pedestal. He dumped the plant on the floor, spilling dirt everywhere. He dug through the dirt, searching for the jewel.

"Nope! No ruby here!"

Rookie ran to the next part of the set, which was decorated to look like a hotel lobby. He grabbed the potted plant from next to the check-in desk. Then he dumped it on the floor and started to dig through the roots.

"Not here either!" he said, brushing the dirt from his flippers. "But I feel like I'm getting close."

He ran into the next room, Miss Ruby's living room. He found a potted plant by the couch and dumped it onto the floor, just like the others. Dirt flew everywhere. Rookie frantically dug through the dirt once more.

While Rookie looked for the jewel, a yellow penguin wearing a director's cap came into the theatre. The actors playing Miss Ruby, Tenor and Jacques Hammer were on the side of the stage, laughing.

"What's going on?" the director asked. "Who is this guy?"

"I'm not sure," Miss Ruby replied. "But he's hilarious!"

Back on stage, Rookie sat on the floor, discouraged. "No ruby! What do I do now?"

The pink penguin he had seen by the costume trunk earlier walked up to him. "Excuse me, are you looking for this?" she asked.

She opened a flipper to reveal a shiny red ruby! It wasn't real, of course. It was a prop for the play. But Rookie still didn't realize that.

"That's it!" Rookie cried, jumping up. "Where did you get it?"

"It got dirty during rehearsal yesterday, so I was cleaning it," she explained. "I was just going to put it back in Miss Ruby's safe."

"Oh, so it was all a misunderstanding!" Rookie said, taking it from her. "Let me take this back to Miss Ruby!"

Rookie bounded across the stage and happily gave the ruby back to the actress playing Miss Ruby.

"Here you go, ma'am," he said. "It wasn't stolen after all."

"Um, thank you," Miss Ruby said, taking the ruby from him.

"No need to thank me," Rookie replied. "That's my job!"

Then he waddled off the stage, feeling great. He couldn't wait to tell his friends at the EPF!

Back at headquarters, the first agent Rookie found was Dot, the agency's master of covert operations.

"Dot, you'll never guess what just happened!" Rookie said excitedly. "I just solved a mystery!"

"Really?" Dot asked. "What happened?"

"I heard that a penguin named Miss Ruby lost her ruby over at The Stage, so I helped her find it," Rookie said.

Dot gasped. "Oh, Rookie, I think I know what happened."

"What do you mean?" Rookie asked.

"Meet me at The Stage in an hour," she said. "Then you'll understand."

When Rookie and Dot got to The Stage, dressed-up penguins were buying tickets to get inside. The play was about to start.

"So why are we back here?" Rookie asked.

Dot pointed up to the sign. "Rookie, you didn't solve a real mystery. You got mixed up in a rehearsal for the play."

Rookie looked up. "Now Showing. Ruby and the Ruby," he read out loud, and his green cheeks turned pink with embarrassment. "So that's why everyone seemed so confused."

Dot put a flipper on his shoulder. "Don't feel bad, Rookie. You were trying to do a good thing. Come on, let's go watch the play."

"All right," Rookie said with a sigh.

The lights were dimming as Dot and Rookie found their seats. Then the bright stage lights switched on to reveal Jacques Hammer sitting behind his desk.

"My name's Hammer. Jacques Hammer," he said. "I was working late. A terrible storm was raging."

There was a knock on the door, and a penguin entered – but it wasn't Miss Ruby. It was a green penguin with a propeller cap and sunglasses.

"Hi," the penguin said. "I'm Rookie."

Dot gasped. "Rookie!" she whispered. "It looks like they've made you a character in the play!"

The director had loved watching Rookie so much that he rewrote the play at the last minute. Rookie watched as the actor playing him played blindfolded hopscotch and dumped all of the potted plants onto the floor. The audience roared with laughter.

"Fantastic!" said a penguin behind Rookie. "They turned an old-fashioned crime drama into a comedy!"

When the play ended, every penguin in the theatre stood up and clapped. Dot turned to Rookie and smiled.

"What do you think of that, Rookie?" Dot asked. "You're a hit!"

Rookie smiled back. "I give it two flippers up!" he replied.

Classified Code

Equipment:
White paper
Wax paper
A pen
Crayons
Your own secret code
Your orders:
Work with a parent or guardian.

1.
Put a sheet of paper on top of a sheet of wax paper.

2.
Use the pen to write a top secret message to another EPF agent. The message must show up on the wax paper so press the pen hard.

3.

Take the wax paper sheet to your fellow agent. You may need to go in disguise.

4.

To reveal the message, your fellow agent must colour the wax paper sheet with a crayon. When the secret message appears, he must decode it.

hi

5. These instructions will self-destruct in 5... 4... 3... 2...

Secret Shadows

Match the Club Penguin character to his or her shadow.

1. **Sensei**

2. **Rockhopper**

3. **Cadence**

4. **Herbert**

5. **Aunt Arctic**

Capture Herbert

G has a lock on Herbert's coordinates. Two agents have set out to capture the polar bear. Which one will succeed? Follow each agent's glowing line to work out which one leads to Herbert.

How to Draw an EPF Agent

With these top secret tips, you can draw your own penguin EPF Agent!

You can start drawing your EPF agent with some basic shapes.

1. Draw two circles, like a snowman - a big circle at the bottom, and a smaller one at the top. Then connect the two circles by making an egg shape around them. Give it a try!

2. Next up: the eyes and beak! Draw a line across his head, and then add the eyes just above it. Then add his beak as a squashed circle underneath.

3. Add a line to the beak for the agent's mouth. A straight line shows that the agent means business!

4. Time to give the EPF agent feet! Make two triangles underneath the bottom of the penguin's body. Think of it like drawing two slices of pizza. But instead of your triangles having sharp corners, round them off a little.

5. Give your EPF Agent arms. To make sure you place them correctly, draw a lightly dotted line from left to right underneath the beak. The shoulders of your penguin's arms will start at this dotted line you drew. To make the arm on the right, start at the dotted line you drew, and add two lines going down and coming to a point, like a very long triangle. For the other arm, start at the dotted line again. This time, make a swooping motion down towards your penguin's tummy to make the arm bend. Then make another line to complete that arm, and you've got it!

6. This agent will be dressed in a classic look - a shirt, jacket and tie. Draw a low swooping line at his neck to start the shirt. Add two triangles to the middle of it for the collar. In the middle of the triangles, draw the shape of the tie hanging down.

7. Next, on each of the penguin's wrists, draw two lines to show the cuffs of his jacket. Draw lines up the arms for the sleeves, and add in the border of his jacket. Remember to add a straight line below his tie to show the bottom of his shirt.

8. All of these lines have been guide lines. Artists draw these to help them with the shape of their drawings. Once you're happy with your guide lines, draw over your agent with darker lines, erase any left-over guide lines, and you're done!

And there you have it - your very own EPF agent! Now that you've learned how, you can draw him going on all kinds of missions. Keep practising on these pages.

Field-Ops Board Game

Many strange things are happening on the island. G needs all agents out in force to investigate. Be the first player to finish all of the Field-Ops to win.

1 START

2 Find an enemy signal coming from the Ski Mountain. Move ahead two spaces.

3 Investigate the sighting of a suspicious crab at the Cove. Move ahead three spaces.

4

16

15 While trying to fix Astro Barrier you accidentally break Thin Ice. Go back five spaces.

14 Rookie is hungry. Stop at the Pizza Parlor for lunch. Lose a turn.

13 Jet Pack Guy lends you his jet pack. Take another turn.

17 Create a signal at the Iceberg. Move forward four spaces.

18 Find the missing parts from the Clock Tower. Move ahead four spaces.

19 Herbert sends you on a wild goose chase on Cart Surfer. Lose a turn.

20 Mysterious tyre tracks lead to a dead end. Go back four spaces.

48

What You'll Need:
- One six-sided dice
- Game pieces: you can use a different coloured jellybean for each player, or a different coin.

5
Rookie accidentally drops your Spy Phono in a barrel of cream soda. Lose a turn.

6
Repair the EPF antenna. Move ahead four spaces.

7
Get lost in the Forest after testing G's new sled. Go back four spaces.

8
Break the mysterious code transmitting from the Beach. Move ahead two spaces.

12
Lose the blueprints to G's latest invention. Go back two spaces.

11
Look after four secret files for G. Move ahead four spaces.

10

9
Change the light bulb at the Beacon before the light goes out. Move ahead two spaces.

21
Deactivate Herbert's computer. Move ahead one space.

22
Finish.
Thanks for keeping Club Penguin safe!

How to Play:
Choose a game piece. Let the youngest player roll first, and then follow the directions on each square. **First player to land on or past the finish line wins!**

49

System Defenders

"It's the best day ever!" Rookie said with a big smile. "Me and my best friend, Jet Pack Guy, are getting pizza together. I'm going to get a chocolate-covered broccoli pizza. Do you want to share it?" he asked the red penguin next to him.

Jet Pack Guy frowned "Negative on that. And Rookie, we work together. I wouldn't say we're best friends."

Rookie didn't even hear Jet Pack Guy's comment. The green penguin had rushed off so quickly that his propeller cap began to spin. He skidded to a stop in front of the Coffee Shop and stuck his head in the door.

"Look at all these brown puffles!" he called.

Jet Pack Guy glanced around. He had noticed that many penguins were walking their brown puffles today. Jet Pack Guy walked to the Coffee Shop door and peeked inside.

Penguins sat on the red couches while other penguins, wearing green aprons, served them hot cocoa. Brown puffles filled the room, helping the servers pour the drinks. The puffles wore goggles and poured hot cocoa from beakers.

"That looks like fun!" Rookie said. He rushed into the crowded room. "I'm going to help -" Before he could finish, he tripped over a bag of java beans.

Jet Pack Guy helped Rookie off the floor with a sigh. "Come on, Rookie. Let's go get that pizza."

They left the Coffee Shop, and as they walked through the Snow Forts and the Plaza, they noticed more penguins waddling around with brown puffles. Some were having snowball fights at the Snow Forts with their puffles. Others were performing at The Stage.

"Interesting," Jet Pack Guy said in a low voice. He approached a blue penguin wearing a t-shirt that said "I Heart My", and had a picture of a brown puffle underneath the letters.

"Excuse me," he said. "Would you please tell me why there are so many brown puffles out today?"

"Sure!" the blue penguin answered enthusiastically. "All the brown puffle fans decided to have a special day. We're calling it 'Take Your Brown Puffle to Work Day'."

Jet Pack Guy nodded. "Got it. Thank you."

"Pizza, pizza, pizza!" Rookie sang. "I'm going to eat a pizza made by a brown puffle. Yum!"

They walked into the Pizza Parlor. Brown puffles were flipping dough in the air like pros.

They ordered their pizza and just as the waiter placed it in front of them, their Spy Phones began blinking. It was a message from G! It said:

"Report to the EPF Command Room at once. I've detected unusual activity on the EPF computers and have traced it to the Ultimate Protobot."

Rookie looked longingly at the hot, cheesy pizza in front of him. "I'm sooooo hungry!"

"We'll eat when we're finished protecting Club Penguin," Jet Pack Guy said sternly. "It's our duty."

"Goodbye, pizza," Rookie said sadly before they teleported to the Command Room using their Spy Phones. "I'll miss you!"

They appeared out of thin air in the Command Room. "I guess secret agents decided to take their puffles to work, too," Rookie said as he looked around. "Look at all of them - they're so cute!"

The high-tech room was filled with computers and monitors. It was also filled with penguin agents and their brown puffles. Some of the puffles were riding on their toy rocket ships. Others were playing with tiny ray beam devices.

"We don't have time for cute," Jet Pack Guy said. "We've got work to do."

He nodded across the room, to where Gary the Gadget Guy was standing next to System Defender, the computer program designed to keep the EPF computers safe. The blue penguin wore round glasses and a white lab coat, and he was frowning.

Rookie followed Jet Pack Guy and they approached Gary.

"Thank you for coming so quickly, agents," said Gary - who was also known by his EPF codename, G.

"You got it, G!" Rookie beamed. "You tell me to jump, I say 'how high'? You ask me to sing, I ask 'how loud'? You tell me to dance -"

G interrupted him. "That's very nice, Rookie. But we've got an emergency to deal with! I've picked up a powerful - and familiar - enemy computer signal. I traced it back to the Ultimate Protobot!"

Jet Pack Guy clenched his flippers. "That bucket of bolts?" he asked gruffly.

A pink penguin standing nearby leaned in. Her brown puffle was perched on her shoulder.

"I'm sorry, I don't mean to eavesdrop," she said. "But I'm a new agent and I don't know who - or what - the Ultimate Protobot is."

"It is one of the greatest threats to the safety of Club Penguin," Gary explained. "The Ultimate Protobot is a robot that wants to destroy the island. Protobot knows that the EPF is the only one who can stop it. That's why it keeps trying to attack our computer systems."

"We kept it from wrecking the island a couple of years ago," Jet Pack Guy added. "We thought we destroyed it. But it is still able to attack computers, making them go haywire."

Gary pressed a few buttons on the System Defender computer. "This is what the Ultimate Protobot looks like," he said.

The face of a metal, robotic penguin filled the screen. Menacing eyes glared from its dome-shaped head. Its steel beak looked like a metal trap.

"Ahhhhhhh!" Rookie cried. He covered his eyes with his flippers.

Jet Pack Guy shook his head. "Get it together, Rookie," he said.

Rookie took a deep breath. "Sorry. That Ultimate Protobot creeps me out. I'd rather hang out with a cute puffle, like yours," he said, nodding to the pink penguin.

She smiled. "Thanks! I think he's pretty cute, too. His name is Chester."

The little brown puffle was holding a ray beam device. He smiled at Rookie.

"Aren't you cute?" Rookie smiled. He forgot all about the Ultimate Protobot as he watched the puffle play.

"That ray beam device is so cool!" he reached out a flipper for it. "Can I try it?"

The brown puffle's eyes grew wide, while the pink penguin looked worried. "I wouldn't touch that if I were you. Chester's been tinkering with it. I'm not sure what it can do."

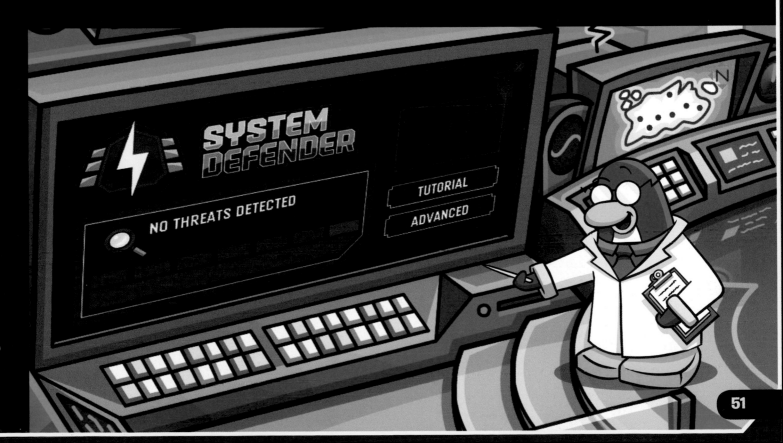

SYSTEM DEFENDER

NO THREATS DETECTED

TUTORIAL

ADVANCED

"I can figure it out," Rookie said confidently as he went to grab the device. The brown puffle tried to skip away from him. Rookie reached out with a flipper, lost his balance, and started to fall.

"Argh!" he yelled. Jet Pack Guy rushed to steady him. Rookie grabbed on to his tie and they both went crashing to the floor.

The brown puffle got out of the way just in time, but it dropped its ray beam. Rookie shook his head as he sat up. "Ouch!" he said. He pulled out the ray beam from underneath him.

"Hey, which way does this go?" he said. Jet Pack Guy sat up next to him. Rookie had the beam pointed at both of them.

"Don't push that button!" Jet Pack Guy yelled.

"Do you mean this button?" Rookie asked as he tapped a red button on the ray beam.

A bright beam of light shot out of it, hitting Rookie and Jet Pack Guy. They squinted against the bright glow. It slowly faded and they both stood, blinking, until they could see again.

Jet Pack Guy looked around. They weren't in the Command Room any more. It was much darker. They were surrounded by wires and some kind of machinery. A loud, electronic humming could be heard.

"What happened? Where are we?" Rookie asked as he looked around.

Jet Pack Guy gritted his teeth. "You happened. I told you not to hit that button."

Rookie looked down at the floor. "I'm sorry. I wanted to find out what that ray beam could do."

"It did something," Jet Pack Guy said. "But I'm not exactly sure what yet."

They were in the middle of what looked to be a long, curving hallway.

"This would be a great space for roller skating!" Rookie said happily. "I wish I had worn my skates today."

Jet Pack Guy let out a groan.

"I really am sorry," Rookie said. "I'll fix this. I know I can help!" He went running down the hall before Jet Pack Guy could stop him.

Jet Pack Guy took out his Spy Phone. He tried getting a signal but couldn't. Suddenly, he heard yelling and the pounding of feet. Rookie was coming back, racing as fast as he could!

"AAAAAAHHHHHHHH!" he yelled as he barrelled down the hall. Something was chasing him!

Red, robot-like creatures stomped down the passage, following Rookie. A red light flashed on top of each robot's

200

50   125   200   500

52

head and sharp teeth filled every mouth. Crash! Rookie collided into Jet Pack Guy, sending them both flying. Jet Pack Guy jumped to his feet and saw a long line of robots marching towards them. He checked for exits. There was nowhere to go. He had to come up with a plan, and fast!

He quickly looked around for a way out, and then he noticed the flipper-sized holes that studded the walls. "We can climb up these walls using the holes!" he told Rookie. "I'll give you a boost."

He helped a shaking Rookie off the floor and gave him a push. The young agent scrambled up the wall and Jet Pack Guy followed.

"Agents? Are you there? Can you hear me?" G's voice filled the room, but it sounded loud and booming, like thunder.

"G? Is that you? Save me!" Rookie yelled.

Jet Pack Guy remained calm, as always. "We're here, G. Go ahead."

"I've ascertained that the brown puffle's ray beam was actually a shrinking device," G explained. "You've both been shrunk to the size of a computer chip."

Rookie looked confused. "Where are we then? On the floor?"

"No, you are both inside the System Defender computer program," G said. "I had it open when the ray beam went off. You were not only shrunk, but teleported into the computer. I believe it is because you both were carrying your Spy Phones. The beam activated the teleporting device, and since the computer was the closest object, that's where you went. But don't panic. I'm working on reversing the beam. I should have you out soon."

Rookie smiled. "What a relief! But what about those red robots that were chasing us?"

Just then, a strange, buzzing sound filled the air.

"BZZZZZK. SYSTEMS ONLINE. BEGIN OPERATION: DESTROY ELITE PENGUIN FORCE," a robotic voice said.

"It's the Ultimate Protobot!" G said. "It's attacking the agency's computers. Agents, it's up to you to stop it from the inside. You'll have to work fast."

"Roger, G. Can you give us further instructions?" Jet Pack Guy asked.

The eerie, robotic voice filled the room again.

Ultimate Protobot

"COMMUNICATIONS INTERCEPTED. SURRENDER NOW. THIS IS YOUR FINAL CHANCE."

Jet Pack Guy shouted, "We're not going down without a fight!"

"That's right!" Rookie yelled. "Secret agents never surrender!"

The robotic voice grew silent.

"Those weren't robots chasing you, they were computer bots sent to infect the computer's mainframe," Jet Pack Guy said. "We've got to stop them."

"I can build cannons!" Rookie said eagerly. "Cannons can destroy bots. I've just got to find them." He went running along the wall, searching through the wires and computer chips for something they could use. He untangled a knot of wires, revealing several red, yellow and purple cannons underneath.

Jet Pack Guy looked over the cannons. "We'll start with the red ones, since we know the red bots are attacking. Red bots usually attack in large groups, and the red cannons are fast. They should be able to blast all of them."

"I'll do it!" Rookie rushed in, scooping up an armful of red cannons. "I'll just put them in the slots in the wall."

He scurried over to the wall slots, shoving in cannons as quickly as he could.

"Do I need to push a button or something?" he asked Jet Pack Guy, who was sorting through the rest of the cannons.

"No. They have auto sensors. When the bots pass in front of them, they'll shoot," Jet Pack Guy explained.

Rookie leaned over the wall.

"Here they come!" he said.

The red bots marched along. They passed the first red cannon. Nothing happened.

"Something's wrong!" Rookie cried. He ran over to the red cannon. It shot a rapid, pulsing beam right at him.

"Woah!" Rookie jumped to get out of the way. He wobbled as he stood on top of the wall.

Jet Pack Guy came rushing over. "You've got them in backwards!" he yelled. "Look out!"

Rookie had jumped in front of another cannon. It shot a laser beam at him. He started to fall off the wall, right on top of the red bots!

Jet Pack Guy quickly launched into action. He switched on his jet pack and flew off the wall, grabbing Rookie before he could crash land into the bots.

"That was a close one. Thanks!" Rookie said. "Now let's fix those cannons!"

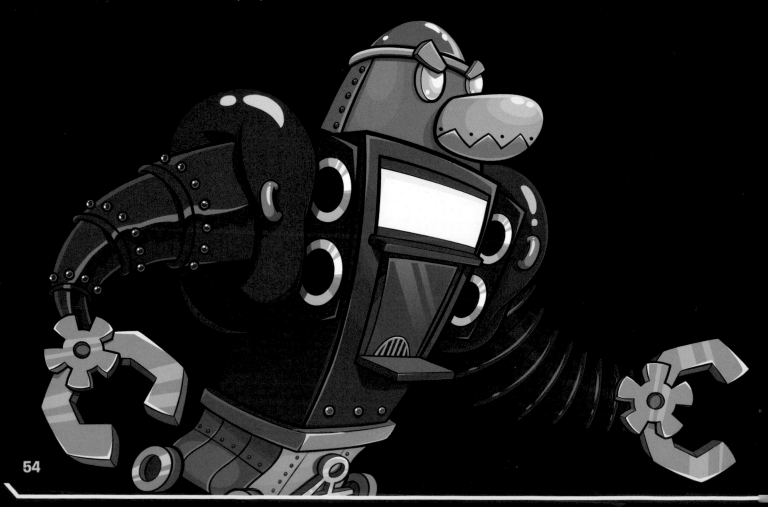

Using his jet pack, Jet Pack Guy flew next to the cannons, holding Rookie in the air while he turned them around. They flew back to the top of the wall to wait.

The red bots continued to march by, but this time they were blasted to bits by the red cannons!

"SCANNING ENEMY DEFENCE. LAUNCHING NEW ATTACK PATTERNS," the Ultimate Protobot said.

"I'm detecting lots of fast enemies," G's voice said. "Just in time! I've only just managed to re-establish communication to warn you. Make sure you have yellow cannons to deal with the yellow bots!"

Rookie and Jet Pack Guy worked quickly to fill in more slots with yellow cannons. The yellow bots, with their big, vacant eyes, came swarming past. They were fast – but not fast enough for the wide-range yellow cannons. Blast! Boom! The bots were defeated.

"COMMENCING ATTACK PATTERN GAMMA." The Ultimate Protobot was launching a new attack.

G's voice filled the air. "I'm picking up purple bot enemy signals. These bots are more powerful. Use purple cannons to finish them off."

"Purple bots are slow, but they can take a lot of damage," Jet Pack Guy said "But they're no match for the powerful purple cannons. We'll teach that rusty tin can a lesson!"

Purple bots with glowing eyes and sharp spikes slowly invaded the computer. Jet Pack Guy and Rookie were ready for them. They had packed purple cannons into the walls.

A purple bot slowly rolled past. ZAP! A ray shot from the purple cannon, evaporating the bot. More purple bots rolled through the hall, but the cannons zapped them one by one until there were none left.

"BZZZK. ERROR. ERROR. WARNING. SYSTEM FAILURE," the Ultimate Protobot said.

"Nice work, agents!" G called. "The Ultimate Protobot's forces are retreating."

"We did it!" Rookie held up his flipper to Jet Pack Guy. "High-five!"

Jet Pack Guy slapped flippers with Rookie and smiled. "I'm glad, G, but how about getting us out of here?"

"I'm working on it," G replied.

Suddenly, a strange rumbling sound filled the air. Were more bots attacking?

"Sorry," Rookie said as he grabbed his belly. "I might have been shrunk, but my stomach wasn't. I'm still hungry!"

"Agents, are you ready? I can now transport you out of the computer and restore you to your normal size."

"Let's do it!" Jet Pack Guy said.

A blast of light filled the room, knocking both Jet Pack Guy and Rookie to the ground. When the light faded, they were in the Command Room again.

G was standing over them, looking concerned. "Are you alright?"

Rookie grinned. "Just hungry!"

"You've worked hard. Go to the Pizza Parlor," G said. "But please stay away from the Pizzatron 3000. I'm really not up to dealing with any more emergencies today."

"You got a deal, G," Rookie said as he looked at Chester, the brown puffle. "As long as Chester promises to keep his shrink ray away from my pizza!"

Draw Your Own EPF Scene

Secret Agent Exam

Alright, agents. In this book you've learned everything you need to know to succeed in the EPF. Did you pay attention when you were reading? Take this quiz to find out.

1 **Where is the Everyday Phoning Facility located?**

a. Town
b. The Ski Village
c. The Iceberg
d. The Plaza

2 **In the story 'Rookie and the Ruby', what is the name of the detective?**

a. Miss Ruby
b. Tenor
c. Jacques Hammer
d. Mickey Wrench

3 **What is EPF agent Dot's greatest talent?**

a. Master of disguise
b. Communications expert
c. Puffle expert
d. Gadget inventor

4 **In the story 'System Defenders', who attacks the EPF computer system?**

a. The Director
b. Herbert
c. Rookie
d. Ultimate Protobot

5 **How do agents know when to report for new Field-Ops?**

a. It's in the Club Penguin Times.
b. They get a Spy Phone message.
c. They go to the Everyday Phoning Facility.
d. They get a secret message on their pizza.

6 **What kind of agent uses Dark Vision Goggles?**

a. Tactical agent
b. Comm agent
c. Stealth agent
d. Tech agent

7 **In the story 'A Mix-Up in the Mine', what is the reason the mine cart isn't working?**

a. It fell apart.
b. One of the wheels had a loose bolt.
c. Herbert greased the tracks.
d. There has been a power cut.

8 **Which Club Penguin resident is known by the secret code name of 'G'?**

a. Gary the Gadget Guy
b. Aunt Arctic
c. Cadence
d. Captain Rockhopper

9 **What type of agent uses a Sat-Pack?**

a. Tactical agent
b. Comm agent
c. Stealth agent
d. Tech agent

10 **Which ocean-dwelling minion helps out Herbert P. Bear with his evil plans?**

a. Ollie the Octopus
b. Sammy the Seahorse
c. Larry the Lobster
d. Klutzy the Crab

Congratulations!

You have proven yourself to be a highly-trained agent by completing all the challenges in this book. The island is a safe place thanks to agents such as yourself!

But remember, your job is not over. As an EPF agent, there is always work to be done. Be on the alert for any strange happenings on the island. Be sure to check your Spy Phone regularly for messages. Keep your agent skills sharp with training.

Thank you for all the hard work you have done and will continue to do to protect Club Penguin. More excitement and adventure awaits. Be prepared!

Answers

10. Spot the Differences

12. Mystery Maze

13. Put Your Memory to the Test

1 - 3; 2 - Mancala; 3 - Orange; 4 - Blue; 5 - Red; 6 - 4; 7 - Happy;
8 - 2; 9 - No; Bonus question - Red.

15. Puffle Puzzle

26. EPF Crossword

27. Word Search

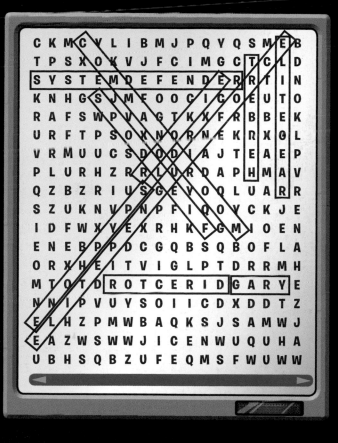

28. Agent Anagrams

GRAY=Gary; LAWN SLOB=snowball; NINE PUGS=penguins; FLEA PUNCH FLU=Puffle Launch; CURTAIN CAT = Aunt Arctic; SEEN IS = Sensei; CHOICE KEY = ice hockey; SOFTER=Forest; FROST=forts; EAGER TILE = Elite Gear

30. Pass Code Puzzle

Spicy squid pizza, extra seaweed.

32. Masters of Disguise

1. Aunt Arctic
2. Gary the Gadget Guy
3. Rockhopper
4. Sensei
5. Cadence

42. Secret Shadows

1. Sensei
2. Rockhopper
3. Cadence
4. Herbert
5. Aunt Arctic

43. Capture Herbert

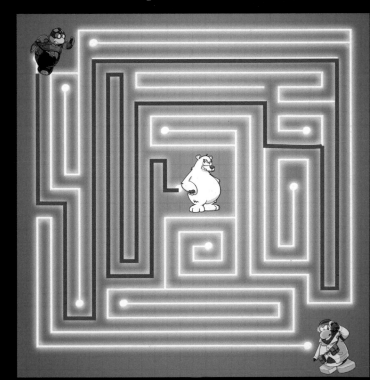

58. Secret Agent Exam

1. B; 2. C; 3. A; 4. D; 5. B; 6. C; 7. B; 8. A; 9. B; 10. D.

Other Club Penguin titles available

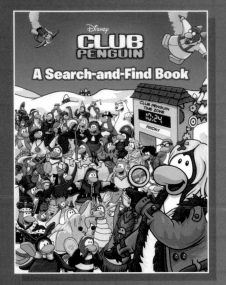

A Search-and-Find Book

ISBN: 9781409390619

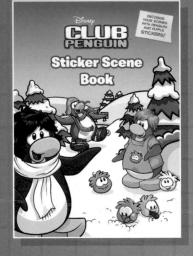

Sticker Scene Book

ISBN: 9781409390480

Meet the Crew

ISBN: 9781409390992

Party Time, All the Time!

ISBN: 9781409390626

Comic Storybook

ISBN: 9781409390473

Official Guide Vol 2

ISBN: 9781409390190